Bryce Canyon National Park

by Jennifer Hackett

Content Consultant

Nanci R. Vargus, Ed.D.
Professor Emeritus, University of Indianapolis

Reading Consultant

Jeanne M. Clidas, Ph.D.
Reading Specialist

Children's Press®
An Imprint of Scholastic Inc.

Library of Congress Cataloging-in-Publication Data

Names: Hackett, Jennifer, author.
Title: Bryce Canyon National Park/by Jennifer Hackett.
Description: New York: Children's Press, an Imprint of Scholastic Inc., 2019. |
Series: Rookie National Parks | Includes bibliographical references and index.
Identifiers: LCCN 2018023400| ISBN 9780531133187 (library binding: alk.
paper) | ISBN 9780531137215 (pbk.: alk. paper)
Subjects: LCSH: Bryce Canyon National Park (Utah)—Juvenile literature. |
National parks and reserves—United States—Juvenile literature.
Classification: LCC F832.B9 H33 2018 | DDC 979.2/52—dc23

Produced by Spooky Cheetah Press
Design: Ed LoPresti Graphic Design
Creative Direction: Judith E. Christ for Scholastic Inc.

Published in 2019 by Children's Press, an imprint of Scholastic Inc.

Printed in Heshan, China 62

SCHOLASTIC, CHILDREN'S PRESS, ROOKIE NATIONAL PARKS™, and
associated logos are trademarks and/or registered trademarks of Scholastic Inc.

1 2 3 4 5 6 7 8 9 10 R 28 27 26 25 24 23 22 21 20 19

Scholastic, Inc., 557 Broadway, New York, NY 10012.

Photos Credits cover: MJFelt/iStockphoto; back cover: bmswanson/iStockphoto; "Ranger Red
Fox" by Bill Mayer for Scholastic; 1-2: Cleo Design/Shutterstock; 3: Robin Runck/Dreamstime;
4-5: Ron Reznick/VW Pics/UIG/Getty Images; 6-7: Richard Maschmeyer/Design Pics/Getty
Images; 8-9: A Held/age fotostock; 10-11 background: Eleanor Scriven/robertharding/Getty
Images; 11 inset: Michael Weber/imageBROKER/age fotostock; 12-13: Nicholas Krotki/
iStockphoto; 14: Andrew Peacock/Getty Images; 15: David H. Carriere/Getty Images; 16-17:
Robin Whalley/Alamy Images; 18-19 background: Michael Zysman/Dreamstime; 19 top inset:
J M Barres/age fotostock; 19 bottom inset: Felix Junker/EyeEm/Getty Images; 20: Panther
Media GmbH/Alamy Images; 21: Chris Mattison/NPL/Minden Pictures; 22-23: David Welling/
NPL/Minden Pictures; 24-25 background: Westend61/Getty Images; 25 inset: Reinhard Eisele/
Mauritius/Superstock, Inc.; 26 left: George Sanker/NPL/Minden Pictures; 26 center top: Wang
LiQiang/Shutterstock; 26 top right: Robert Royse/BIA/Minden Pictures; 26 center bottom:
Design Pics/Superstock, Inc.; 26 bottom right: Joel Sartore/Getty Images; 27 top left: Eric
Meola/Getty Images; 27 top right: fivespots/Shutterstock; 27 bottom left: Duncan Usher/
ardea.com/age fotostock; 27 bottom center: Isselee/Dreamstime; 27 bottom right: GlobalP/
iStockphoto; 30 top left: Gregory G Dimijian/Getty Images; 30 top right: Cyrus McCrimmon/
The Denver Post/Getty Images; 30 bottom left: © Lee Dittmann, used with permission; 30
bottom right: NatPar Collection/Alamy Images; 31 top: LordRunar/Getty Images; 31 center
bottom: Russ Bishop/Stock Connection/Aurora Photos; 31 bottom: EQRoy/Shutterstock; 31
center top: Michael Zysman/Dreamstime; 32: gary718/Shutterstock.

Maps by Jim McMahon/Mapman ®

Table of Contents

Welcome to Bryce Canyon National Park!

Bryce Canyon is in Utah. It became a **national park** in 1928. People visit national parks to explore nature.

The most popular part of the park is its large **amphitheater**. Bryce also has many rocky towers. They were created by millions of years of **erosion**.

I am Ranger Red Fox, your tour guide. Are you ready for an amazing adventure in Bryce Canyon?

United States

Utah

Bryce Canyon
National Park

N
W · E
S

Visitors can hike around the park or take in the sights on horseback. Many start the day at Sunrise Point and end it at Sunset Point. Can you guess why?

The Queens Garden Trail is a popular hike.

Chapter 1

Rocks That Rock

Millions of years ago, this area was just flat rocks.

Over many years, natural forces like wind and water wore away the rock. The flat landscape was turned into the open areas and tall rocky towers we see today in Bryce.

Eventually, erosion turned those rocky towers into wavy rock pillars. They are called *hoodoos*. Hoodoos are natural works of art.

Bryce Canyon has the most hoodoos of any place in the world.

One of the most famous hoodoos in Bryce Canyon is Thor's Hammer. Visitors get up early to watch the sun rise over the towering rock pillar.

Thor's Hammer is about 150 feet (46 meters) tall.

You can see about three times as many stars in Bryce as anywhere else in the world!

The Rim Trail winds about 5 miles (8 kilometers) around the amphitheater.

Chapter 2

Traveling the Trails

There are two ways to explore Bryce—from up high and down low.

Visitors hiking the Rim Trail can get a bird's-eye view of the park. On a clear day, it's possible to see for 100 miles (161 kilometers)! At night, 7,500 stars can be seen shining in the sky.

Many visitors like to hike deep down into the park. The Mossy Cave Trail leads to waterfalls and underground springs.

Hikers on the Mossy Cave Trail might also see hoodoo graveyards.

These mounds are all that remain of hoodoos that have been worn away by erosion.

hoodoo graveyard

The Mossy Cave Trail is one of the few trails with waterfalls in Bryce Canyon.

Running water can wear away hoodoos.

Bryce Canyon is dry and rocky. But it has forests full of trees.

Chapter 3

Plants and Trees

Bryce Canyon National Park is so tall from top to bottom that it has different **climate** zones. The canyon rim gets plenty of sun and water. Down at the bottom, it is hot and very dry. Visitors can discover a variety of plants and trees in these different areas.

The park's oldest trees are highest up where there's the most sun and water. These include firs, aspens, and bristlecone pines.

Some bristlecone pine trees are 1,600 years old!

Ponderosa pines and manzanita trees are found farther down. Plants that don't need much water, like cactus and juniper, live at the bottom.

manzanita tree

prickly pear cactus

The California condor is the largest bird of prey in the United States.

Chapter 4

Wild About Wildlife

Almost 250 types of animals call Bryce Canyon home. Deer and porcupines scurry among the hoodoos. Condors and peregrine falcons soar overhead. Lizards and tiger salamanders bask in the sun.

tiger salamander

Bryce has the largest population of Utah prairie dogs in the world.

About 200 of these adorable animals live in the park.

Utah prairie dogs are endangered. They are at risk of dying out.

Imagine you
could visit Bryce
Canyon National Park.
What would you
do there?

People visit Bryce Canyon for many reasons. Some hike to see hoodoos and wild animals. Others take buses to watch the sunset or to stargaze. Some people snowshoe or ski in winter. There is always so much to see and do in Bryce.

Bryce Canyon is like a whole different park in winter!

Here are some of the amazing animals that live in Bryce Canyon National Park.

peregrine
falcon

willow flycatcher

tiger
salamander

pronghorn
deer

California
condor

Wildlife by the Numbers

The park is home to about...

175 types of birds   **59** types of mammals

The park is home to more than 1,000 different types of bugs.

Utah prarie dog

Great Basin rattlesnake

mule deer

North American porcupine

mountain lion

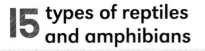

15 types of reptiles and amphibians

0 native fish species

Where Is Ranger Red Fox?

Oh no! Ranger Red Fox has lost his way in the park. But you can help. Use the map and the clues below to find him.

1. Ranger Red Fox got up with the sun to start his day at Sunrise Point.

2. Then he hiked south along the Rim Trail to visit Thor's Hammer.

3. He headed northeast along the Mossy Cave Trail and had a picnic lunch by the waterfall.

4. Finally, he walked southwest to watch the sunset.

Help! Can you find me?

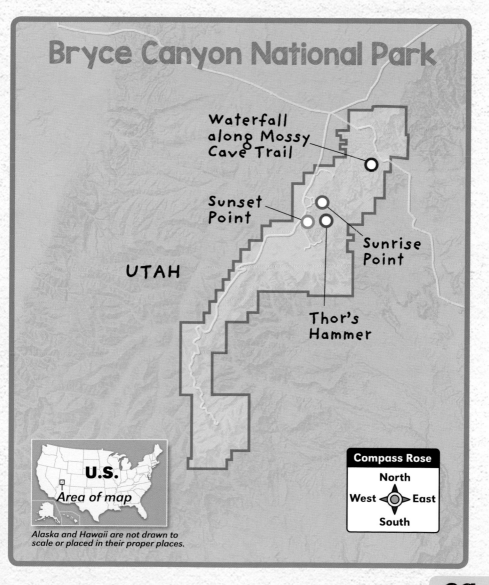

Bryce Canyon National Park

Waterfall along Mossy Cave Trail

Sunset Point

Sunrise Point

Thor's Hammer

UTAH

U.S.
Area of map

Alaska and Hawaii are not drawn to scale or placed in their proper places.

Compass Rose

North

West ◆ East

South

Match each Bryce Canyon wildflower to its name. Read the clues to help you.

A.

1. Bryce Canyon paintbrush
Clue: This wildflower with purple-red petals is found only in Bryce Canyon.

2. Canyon penstemon
Clue: This rare blue flower looks like a tube.

B.

3. Showy stoneseed
Clue: These yellow flowers have a frilly edge to their petals.

C.

4. Western wallflower
Clue: The yellow flowers on this plant have four round petals.

D.

Glossary

amphitheater (am-fi-thee-tur): large open area surrounded by steep sides

climate (**klye**-mit): the weather typical of a place over a long period of time

erosion (i-**roh**-zhuhn): the wearing away of something by water or wind

national park (**nash**-uh-nuhl pahrk): area where the land and its animals are protected by the U.S. government

Index

Facts for Now

Visit this Scholastic Web site for more information
on Bryce Canyon National Park:
www.factsfornow.scholastic.com
Enter the keywords **Bryce Canyon**

About the Author

Jennifer Hackett is a magazine editor for Scholastic MATH. She
loves writing about cool things for kids, especially about science.
Acadia is her favorite national park, but she thinks Bryce Canyon
is pretty cool, too!